HOW TO MAKE HIM WANT YOU

AND FALL IN LOVE WITH YOU

By David Right

PREFACE

Whether you're in a serious relationship with a long term boyfriend, or you've just started playing the dating field again, there are few things that you should always remember in order to make dating a enjoyable and fulfilling experience. Although the perfect relationship can only exist in fairytales, you can easily make your relationship seem like one just by keeping a few tips in mind. Want to know how you can be the best you can be in any relationship you embark on? Then here is a book on relationship advice for women that you shouldn't dare miss.

Relationships need not always end up in tears or heartache so if you dream of living a fairytale story, you need to put effort into it. Don't allow yourself to be the damsel in distress when all it takes to have a perfect relationship are few useful tips that every woman should know.

Contents

CHAPTER 1- UNDERSTANDING MEN IN RELATIONSHIPS

Understanding men, though many women, will disagree, is quite simple. The reason is that men, unlike women, are very simple creatures. They have simple needs, desires, and are not overtly emotional, like women. Still, many women find themselves in a situation where they never get a call after the first date, or where they have been in a series of broken relationships. They have been dumped by men without any warning, or left waiting for marriage proposal, which never comes their way. If you too have faced a familiar situation, here are a few tips for you.

Tips To Understand Men Better

It is human nature, that we always want the things which we cannot have. And once we have them, our desire fades away. Men are pretty much the same. If on the first date itself, a woman comes across as somebody, who is available to a man, whether emotionally or physically, the man may not fantasize about the woman anymore. So, a useful tip for all single women is to remain a mystery for the man, at least in the initial phases of the relationship. It is a bad idea to tell a man how crazy you are for him, or how much you want him. Let him confess his feelings to you initially, be slightly detached, and give him the opportunity to miss you. Once he makes the first move, you can tell him whatever you want to.

Men like challenges in life, and love to 'chase' a woman. So why deny him his fun? Be slightly unpredictable, once in a while. Do not always agree to what he says. Have your own opinions in life. Be very clear about your needs and expectations, and do not overlook them, even if the man asks you to. A modern, assertive, and challenging woman is much more appealing to a man, than a woman who is always complying to her man's wishes.

Men does not like women who cling to them. A woman who makes huge emotional demands to the man, who constantly looks for his attention, and is always trying to please him, is actually driving him away. So, never ever sound desperate to a man, as it is bound to turn him off. The more a woman clings to a man, the more he will try to distance himself from her.

When a man is in love, he will be at his best behavior around the woman he loves. He will do anything to keep her attention to himself. He will try to know about her likes and dislikes, try to understand her better, and also be protective of her.

Strangely, men in love may sometimes act in a very weird manner. He may act detached, all because he is fearful that he is falling in love with one particular woman. At the same time, he can become a little possessive of the woman he loves, because he fears that the woman might leave him for someone else.

Once a man is truly committed, he will introduce his woman to all his friends, family, and everyone he knows. This is a man's way of showing that the woman now belongs to him. Although marriage is something that makes most men jittery, but when the right woman comes along, men no longer feel that way, and are usually ready for commitment.

As you can see, understanding men is not that difficult. They want the same things from a relationship, and have the same insecurities as women do. With a little understanding and care, a woman can easily get whatever she wants from her man.

Mistakes women makes in relationships

Women make mistakes in relationships, knowingly or unknowingly, out of love or out of ego, out of insecurity or just to play mind games. Whatever it may be, making mistakes is human nature and can be controlled. You should learn to deal with these misdoings, that can shake your relationship, for a less complicated future with your better half (yes, less complicated is what I wrote, you cannot be in a relationship free from obstacles or complications, can you?). This book in no way intends to harm the sentiments of ladies, nor does it intend to harm anyone personally, one or the other mistake out of these is made by every woman in a relationship. The male brigade also makes mistakes, no doubt, but following the universal rule of ladies first, let's first pinpoint the mistakes women tend to make in their love life.

Top 10 Mistakes Women Make in Relationships with Men
1. Being Clingy

Do you expect your boyfriend to inform you about his whereabouts every hour? Do you feel the heat of insecurity when he casually talks with other females? You expect him to conduct himself the way you want, and at the worst, you have hired someone to spy over him! If you relate to all this, you are clingy. You are also jealous and overtly possessive. I wish to ask you, what makes you a clingy girlfriend? Being excessively possessive is the first sign of missing trust, the building block of any relationship. Analyze for yourself what is making you so clingy to your boyfriend. Sort out the things as soon as you can, before your guy runs away from you. No man with brains will tolerate a clingy girlfriend.

2. Suspecting for No Valid Reason

Suspecting her guy for small reasons is what alot of female folk do in a relationship. Picture this - When your guy is out-of-town and calls you, you hear a female voice in the background. Suspicion starts building and you assume he is dating some other girl in your absence. You fights with him and makes accusations with no concrete evidence. Is this suspicion justified? Your boyfriend, or say, husband, might be helping a girl, considering she is his friend or he is in a business meeting, who knows. So, never fight or suspect if you are not sure. Will it not hamper your relationship? Next time, do suspect and fight, but only if you have a valid proof and are sure that he is indeed cheating.

3. Cheating on Him

Women are known to keep commitments and promises among both the sexes, and that is an universal fact. But the natives of Venus are also humans and can sway on finding a better prospect. You are not happy with the way the bond is shaping up, and are not fully satisfied with your boyfriend, also you do not want to leave him. Your eyes begin to rove, you start flirting in an unhealthy way, and at last, you cheat on him!

The reason for this mistake is - you didn't take the effort to enliven the dying relationship, you failed in the relationship and didn't talk it out with your boyfriend/husband. So, take all the efforts to make the relationship work; if not, ☐uit, but not cheat or be with two persons.

4. Making Unrealistic Demands

Some girls commit this mistake of thinking that their boyfriend is their personal property. More than the guy, they think his wallet is their own. But it is not! Just to know they are being loved, girls start making unrealistic demands from their boyfriends. They become demanding, not realizing that he cannot afford what they demand all the time. A relationship is more about sharing your emotional securities with the other person, it is about supporting each other, it is finding yourself in the other person, rather than making material demands, or using him to fulfilling your motives and wishes. Also, females and males are wired differently hence this big difference in thinking. So, stop expecting him to remember all your anniversaries and birthdays. This one is for your own good.

5. Excess Intrusion

This is somewhat similar to being a clingy girlfriend. Even if you are a staunch believer in - "we are two bodies, one soul", be practical. You two are two distinct individuals with two different bodies and souls, and so you just cannot cross that line the person has set for others, including you. Learn to give each other the re□uired space, and do not excessively intrude in his life. When he says, he needs to be alone, he means it. Give him that independence, and you both will be happy. Know that he loves you, and let him do the things he enjoys doing. Do not force yourself to create a space in the person's life. If he wants you, he will create a big one, for sure.

6. Playing Mind Games

Not everyone in the male tribe is blessed to read the mind of a woman, which is way more complex than solving a Rubik's cube (can't think of anything else!). Do you expect your boyfriend to read your mind, and the poor guy is left guessing? I know it is tempting to play mind games with your guy, or draining him emotionally, but you should better avoid these mind games. Guys, though as unpredictable as the weather, are □uite straightforward and cannot grasp or like these drama queen tactics of emotional wars and tears. So better leave them for your female friends, and do not always expect him to read your mind.

7. Fighting in Public

Note: Even men can start fighting in public. You hear gossip about him involved with someone at the workplace from a source, you trust or do not trust. But without thinking for a second, you give fire to the seething volcano in you. Without finding relevancy of the information, in rage, you storm to his workplace, or any other place, and fight in full public view. Isn't it embarrassing? No matter how angry you are, this cannot be explained or justified. Though you are fighting because you have a point, or because you love, or are deeply hurt, more than anything else, you are providing ideas to gossip mongers to spin stories, and this actually reveals the weak base of your relationship to others around. So, stop providing entertainment to gossip hungry public. Do defend your guy in public, but don't attack or throttle him in public. Bear in mind - You are making a fool of yourself, your partner, and your relationship. This also holds true for show of affection, some guys do not like PDA and so it is better if you do not force him to show his love publicly.

8. Losing Individuality

Are you losing your individuality being with the person? When others talk about you, it is always about you with that person. You cannot make a decision for yourself and end up consulting the person for even a small decision, informing him every little development. Ahhh! Take some time out for yourself girl, you are making a mistake. Yes, you two are together and very much in love, but do not lose your own individuality for that person. Don't depend so much on the person, that if he leaves you tomorrow, you will find it hard to recover for a long time. Be a strong person, pamper yourself with things you like, earn your money, spend it, enjoy with your gal friends; in short be independent and stand up for yourself.

9. Forcing Him for Marriage

If you know he loves you, you should wait for him to make the marriage move. Do not bring up the marriage topic every time you talk, it will turn your guy off, and you would end up wasting time fighting. Instead, wait for that special moment (if you are sure it will come) when your boyfriend proposes to you. You cannot force a person to marry you, it will be a mistake and the marriage would be an unhappy one. This is a common mistake women tend to make in relationships and can be avoided only if you understand your boyfriend.

10. Misreading the Signs

It is a well-known fact that men are more action oriented, as far as the 'expression of love' is concerned. In the initial stages of a relationship, you like the guy. You both go out for a movie and he puts his arms around you or snuggles close to you, when you are together. You misread the signs and conclude that he is into you only physically. But as far as the above signs are concerned, keep in mind, it is his way of showing care and love for you. You better understands the signs; surely you can understand the difference in touch. He may not feel it is necessary to call you everyday or every hour, but he does care; only his way of expressing love is different.

Knowingly or unknowingly these mistakes do occur. And they will haunt men for generations to come. But do take all the efforts to minimize them. You both have to put in e ual effort to make a relationship work; you should learn to compromise, to forgive for some past misdoings. After all, you want to derive some positives from the relationship, and it should not be a burden that will kill and frustrate you each day. So, forget the past, learn to trust, give all your love and stop expecting. Believe me, your relationship would be least complicated.

What men want women to know

Men and women, being polar opposites, have starkly different approaches to life. Women are more vocal when it comes to stating what they want. Ask a man though if he has something to say to his woman and he will cautiously look around, murmur something about the walls having ears, take you to a deadly quiet place where there's no one to overhear, and whisper faintly about some silly things he has to say about the girl he loves or is dating. Women inherently tend to be more open.

Things Men Want Women to Know

Men desire women who assiduously opts for self-improvement by learning things in order to improve their relationship. So if you are one of those women who wants a view into the mind of a man, and learn the things men wish women knew, then you have pick up the right book.

As there are many different things that men would like women to know, this book gives only a general overview of some of them.

About Sex

Most women dismiss all men in general as heartless sexual predators. However, even though we like the act alot, there's more to some of us than just that. We genuinely want to know more about a woman we are out with. We like to connect with a woman mentally.

Nagging

This tops the list of things that women do that we hate. And for some reason, men get nagged alot. First it is our mothers, then it is our women. We know that there are things to be done. We know that we have to clean behind ourselves. So stop telling us and ruining the Super Bowl while we're watching it.

We Love the TV

Although this is common knowledge, we do not love it more than we love you. Sure, we seem to give it a lot more attention, fawn over it, flaunt it, and watch it alot. We might crave for it more when we are away from home or are more addicted to it than anything else in the world, and may even get angry if you switch it off when we are watching it, but we still love you more.

The Other Guy

We absolutely hate any other man hitting on you. Whether we know him or you know him, whether he's your ex boyfriend or some random guy from the street who gives you a second look, we do not like it. We might also get a little violent when someone tries to give you more attention than we can afford to put up with. Men are very competitive by nature, so this extra attention from another man will rule us and make us act more attention-giving. Please do not, however, take advantage of this.

Dress Up

Men love being doted on and showered with attention. We especially love it when you go the extra mile to dress up for us, wear make up, and generally look good when we are with you. Men are more visual creatures and like admiring the beauty of the woman they are with.

Definition of Fun

Our definition of fun is vastly different from yours. Women like shopping and going on a nice date at a good place. Men like going to one of those places you call 'a dump', and watching a game with a hundred other drunk guys. So it is better if we are left to do our own things. One of the things men wish women knew is that going for shopping can be a real chore.

Compliments

Compliment us, I mean to say. Men do like being complimented once in a while and hence it would be nice if you told us how much you love us, or appreciate us for doing something well. For example, if you do not like a gift we got you, just pretend that you do.

Naughty is Nice

Men like it when women get naughty. It does not make us uncomfortable at all. Even a little sexual innuendo on your part is always welcome. Anywhere and anytime. All that is needed is a little indication.

We Hate Games

Football is fine. Basketball works too. Relationship games though, really anger us. We hate them from the bottom of our hearts when you pretend not to love us, when you pretend to ignore us, or when you use sex as a weapon. Some of us know that you're pretending, while others can't tell. Either way, men are simple one-track minded creatures, and dislike complex relationship issues.

Care

We love being taken care of. We love it when you cook for us, when you take us out, when you make us breakfast in bed, and other similar stuff. We like being pampered once in a while. A show of love and care never goes unnoticed. We love it when you're always there to pick up our calls and come out with us, or when you decide to look good for us.

To conclude, I would like to say that, intuitive that women are, they probably know what men want from them; but they always prefer a little confirmation.

Types of men you should not date

We know that the perfect guy does not exist. Yes, nor does the perfect girl! Of course, every guy will have some negative qualities, but there has to be a limit right? There are some types of men that no woman can bear. You might be hopelessly in love with him, but open your eyes, or at least your brains. It is alright to get a little blind in love, but don't be dumb!

So here's your checklist, see if the guy fits into any category here, cause then it's time to say goodbye! And guys who are reading this, if you think you belong to one of the following, please try to mend your ways.

1.The Flirt

He is good-looking and oh-so charming. He knows exactly how to make you fall for him; you and many more! Yes, for the flirt, dating is all about getting maximum girls and then choosing the best options. You can never expect to be a priority with this guy. If he's free on a Friday night, he'll call you, if he has better options he will make up some excuse. We know girl, it is hard to resist those sweeter-than-honey words and twinkling eyes, but remember this boy is trouble. He is just going to play with you till he gets bored. So, either you play with him as well, or just stay away from him altogether!

2.The Obsessed One

He is obsessed with you. He wants to talk to you all day, every day. If you don't meet him, he will show up at your workplace or home, he will ⬚uestion your every move, he will want to know everything about you. Basically, the guy does not know how to give space or respect your personal life. Sharing is good, but when he starts to tell you where to go and where not to, that is too much. He may start getting worked up with your male colleagues or friends, start to object your clothes, and what not. He just wants you, all for himself. This obsession is not cute at all, although it may seems that way first. So get rid of him before he becomes a burden for you.

3.The Guy Who Never Pays

He asked you out for dinner and asked you to pay cause he was short on cash. Okay, you did pay, but what if this happens regularly? Girl, it's time to ditch this loser, who won't even go dutch with you. We are not expecting the guy to pay for all the dates, but at least he can offer or split the bill. This one just wants to have his cake and eat it too!

4.The Mama's Boy

Let me state this first, we don't mean a guy who loves and takes care of his mom is bad. In fact, it's a major turn on. But, there has to be a line, a limit. Every little thing cannot be done according to his mom. Imagine the guy asking his mommy what he should wear or what he should eat or continuously talking on the phone when he is with you. Not cool.

5.The Rebound Guy

This guy is clearly not over his ex, and you are just a distraction for him. Ouch! That hurts, but it is true! He just needs someone to make him forget his dear ex. He will keep comparing your little things with her. Talking about your ex is fine, but obsessing about her, definitely not.

6.The Man Child

The man child or the peter pan simply does not want to grow. He will just live off his parent's money or work just to pay off his bills. He constantly needs you to take care of him. He will behave just like a high school kid, and need you to cook for him and feed him. Basically, dating him is like adopting an overgrown child. Hopefully, you don't want to do that!

7.The Cheater

He has cheated in the past, and he will cheat in the future. There is nothing wrong in giving a second chance to someone you love, but there should be some remorse shown by the guy. If he is just trying to find excuses and is not ready to accept his mistake, then there's seriously no point in being with him. He has an interest in every woman he sets his eye on. Even when he is with you, he will blatantly check out other women. You don't need so much crap girl, ditch him!

8. The Liar

He is a compulsive liar. He will lie about his relationships, career, salary, house, or car. He just wants to paint a rosy picture of his perfect life to impress you. Once you fall for him, little things will start to show up, and you will realize he isn't the guy you fell for, not even close actually. Whatever the reason, lying is not cool. And, you girl, definitely don't deserve this guy.

9. The Commitment Phobic

Ahh, this type is found in abundance. He likes hanging out with you, he loves banging you, but he won't commit to you. He will either have a story about how his heart was broken by some girl or how he had a disturbed childhood. Whatever the reason, unless you are looking for just a fling, do not continue dating him. Everything will seem perfect but you can never have assurance and love from him.

10.The Needy One

Even the thought of this guy is enough to give me the creeps. He is very clingy and will stick to you like a parasite. He will constantly text you, will want to meet you everyday, talk to you all the time, and what not. Come on girl, I am sure you don't have that much patience. Just get rid of him!

11.The Narcissistic

He is probably good-looking or okay-looking, but according to him he is the most handsome guy in the world. He will take more time to get ready than you. He will use a plethora of beauty products to maintain his dashing looks, and he will never take criticism about his appearance in a positive way.

12.The One Who's Never Around

You have to wait for hours for his reply, he will never pick up your phone, and call you back when he pleases. Well, those are danger bells girl. You definitely don't have to be with someone who takes you for granted. Forget feeling special and loved, he isn't even there when you need him the most. He will call you whenever he wants and make plans without talking to you, and if you say no, he will overreact. Why do you even need this guy, just dump him!

CHAPTER 2- DATING ADVICE FOR WOMEN

Every individual has their own reasoning and understanding and they pretty much work accordingly. Some people feel that if they are aware of some dating tips and ideas, it will be productive. I can agree to this up to a point, but then I have my own set of beliefs when it comes to dating (which we will discuss in this article). And since the topic is about giving dating advice, let's just stick to one side of the dating scenario.

Important Tips to Remember

If you're looking for helpful advice for women, the task to categorize different personal situations can be difficult. What I mean to say is that we all have separate lives and are at different junctions. Some of us may have just begun dating, some were married before and are now re-entering the dating scene at a later stage, and looking for specific advice since there are kids involved, etc. In that case, classifying each of these categorizes can become too in-depth and too confusing.

Hence, we will keep this as simple and less confusing as possible. I mean, dating is not rocket science, so why should we make it one? The advice is pretty simple to understand. What women want in a man is a sense of security, love, compassion, and the desire to be with him. The only difference in all these is the age factor; and I don't believe that age can change or alter the advice.

Do ...

Aim at looking "gorgeous". Take a shower right before the date, wear a sexy/cute outfit, and don't forget to accessorize yourself. Knock him down with your killer look.

relax on your dates (initially) and try to have as much fun as possible. Even if you don't like certain activities like bowling, dancing, or anything else, don't get upset and ruin the date.

talk, and make him talk about himself as well. You could be having great conversation topics, but what's the use if only one person is doing all the talking.

Pay him compliments. As much as we love compliments ladies, so do men. Even he must be as nervous as you are on the date. Make him feel relaxed around you and he will love that.

have a positive outlook about things. Don't crib or complain about something excessively. We all like to be around people that are fun and easy to hang out with.

Be honest about things. That goes during and after the date. Let him know that if you're interested, you will call him. And if there isn't any spark between you two, don't keep him hanging.

Flirt with him, make eye contact; show him that you are interested. But also keep air of mystery around yourself (that can turn guys on like anything).

Don't ...

Drink too much or get drunk. It's a huge turn off and won't give him a good impression about yourself.

Call him immediately after the date is over. If you feel that the date went well but he still hasn't called you, call him yourself. Unfortunately, if he doesn't want a second date, let it be. Don't try and chase him or scare him off.

Jump into bed with him. Hold off on getting physically intimate with him till you get to know him a little. Don't jump into bed with a stranger and then regret it later on.

Flirt with other men while you're on a date with him. That's not cool (many women do that) and you really don't want to butcher your chances with this guy.

As I mentioned before, every individual has different re□uirements when it comes to dating. So, getting specific information and tips will only make the process (of dating) much simpler.

Things to talk about on the first date

We always wonder what are the things to ask on a first date. We guess more guys face this □uestion than girls. We may be wrong, but yes, to make your first date fun for both of you, it is important to know what to talk about on a first date. And so, the only thing you need is a conversation starter.

Once the conversation starts and you start feeling more and more at ease with each other, we're sure things will get a lot easier for both of you.

Talking Points for a First Date

You are bustling with topics, but then you face that Socrates-Hamlet-Shakespearean dilemma: to say or not to say. Well, these are some of the topics that fall under the category: to say.

✔ Basic Information

✔ Likes and Dislikes

✔ Funny Stories

✔ 'How Was Your Day?'

- Basic Information

Nothing wrong in sharing basic information about each other. You know, where are you from? What do you do?... All the stuff the Backstreet Boys say they don't care about in the song 'As Long as You Love Me'. OK, maybe that was a bad example, but it's always good to know if you have any friends in common and ensure that you don't have any relatives in common!

- Likes and Dislikes

Another very important thing you'd like to know about your date is their likes and dislikes. Their favorite book, their favorite sport, their favorite band, their favorite song. I've noticed that once you do find something you share in common with someone, you get this nice comfortable feeling that the person is one of your own. In case you don't, keep probing, you'll find something. In case you still don't, you'll have a nice long conversation! Just as long as you don't start arguing as to how the hell they support Manchester United and buzz off all shocked.

- Funny Stories

Funny stories are always some of the best conversation starters. In fact some people always like to have a nice, funny anecdote or a joke up their sleeve to tell on a date or when they're meeting someone new. It really helps break the ice and makes you comfortable that you can make the other person laugh.

- 'How Was Your Day?'

Well often you go out on a date with someone you've known for a while. So you pretty much know all the basic information about them and their likes and dislikes. So what's the point in discussing those? But even when you know them, a date needs a different psychological preparation and hence can get a little awkward. So simply ask them how was their day? what did they do? And the like.

Things You Should Never Talk about on a First Date

Let us discuss the perhaps more important and decidedly gray territory of the first date talk dilemma: what not to say.

✗ Sex

✗ Past Relationships

✗ The Weather

- Sex

Unless of course, it is that sort of date. I still don't know why so many of us can't wrap their heads around the fact that sexual preferences ought to be kept under the wraps, at least for the first date. Flirt, but you have to know where to draw the boundaries where flirting starts getting kinky. Oh, and for the record, it can be uncomfortable for the guy as well and not just the girl on the first date.

- Past Relationships

That's always a bad place to go. But people trying to get over someone or on a rebound date do, talk about their ex like all the time. Which may be fine for some, but a real dampener for most of the people.

- The Weather

Because that's always a very stupid thing to talk about and makes both of you more uncomfortable as you realize that you're not making much headway with your conversation.

Whatever you do, always remember the two most important rules - to be yourself and to just go and enjoy your time out. No point in lying about who you are, cause then you're just impressing your date with someone else and not you. and no use worrying about it either, worrying just makes it worse. Don't worry. Relax. Your date will go just fine!

Biggest turn-off for men on the first date

Men avoid women who ask too many ⬚uestions, are clingy, who don't respect their friends or private time, and those who are high maintenance.

A first date is an exciting concept for both men and women. It is a time when expectations build up and bring along excitement, thrill, and nervousness. It is also really hard to predict how the first meeting would go, and even if it went well, would a second date happen OR this fairy tale might come true and you might end up finding your significant other. Stop! Let's put all these beautiful thoughts aside, especially women, and first let's uncover some of the biggest first date disasters that should be avoided at all costs. Mind you, avoiding these ⬚uirks doesn't guarantee a smooth first or second date, but at least at the end of the day, you can be proud of yourself for doing the best you could and being presentable enough.

Women, Don't do this on a First Date

Appear Unhygienic

Let me put it in simple English - it is a deal-breaker. Poor hygiene is not just a big NO for men, but also for women. Ensure that you have a fresh breath and also look great before you meet each other. Also, make sure that all your nails are trim and carry a decent color. This helps if you are wearing open-toe shoes. Body odor is another important aspect that can't be ignored. Take a bath and do apply a perfume or deodorant, before stepping out. It has been observed that most men who aren't happy after their dates, complain about body odor and bad breath.

Discuss Exes

Again a big turn-off, don't talk about past affairs or how good or bad your recent ex-boyfriend or spouse was. Of course, the topic of past relationships is bound to come up, but it is better to keep it short and brief, and better still, for a later date. Otherwise, he would be searching for the emergency exit. Have a casual tone while discussing your ex. Any aggressiveness in tone or behavior indicates strong feelings for the ex, and is enough to hurt your date's fragile ego.

Crib about Men

This is for those women who think, it is only the fairer sex that faces all of life's hardships, and hold men responsible for every wrong that has happened to them. This also refers to women who criticize men for everything, and also influence other women to act against them. Most men appreciate gender e□uality, but pointing out 100 different reasons that show why women are better than men is certainly a big turn-off, and is just going to scare him away.

Be too Nice

No one was born a saint, and it is too obvious when someone tries too hard to show their good side. Be true to yourself and him, as it isn't healthy to be someone you're not, in the long run. This also doesn't mean that you have to reveal your inner-demons and rattle about your shortcomings all at once. If you are not comfortable with something, then let him know. Be respectful while saying so, and choose appropriate words while talking to your date. In a nutshell, be honest and don't pretend to be someone you're actually not.

Avoid the Bill

Tradition and the 'Dating Rule Book' says men should pay on the first date. However, this theory is not favored by today's men. Of course, he doesn't expect you to pay, but he does expect some politeness and a suggestion of splitting the bill. Remember, it is just the first date, you aren't married yet. So don't expect him to pay the entire bill, be kind enough to chip in some cash, or at least offer to do so. No man is going to ask you to share or pay the bill, but they certainly want you to show that you care.

Drink too Much

Social drinking is an acceptable norm. So, if the guy offers you a drink on your first date, order your mix. However, drink within your limits, for a lady never misbehaves on her first date, or shouldn't in fact. Remember this, a lady in control of herself is more likely to make a lasting impression on the man, than the one who will have to be carried home!

Plan your Future

It is no secret that women love planning their future. However, discussing your desire of having a perfect home, partner, and kids, is certainly too overwhelming for a man on a first date. Contrary to what people assumes, not all men are commitment-phobic. They just don't want their lives decided by someone else, and hence, women who are too anxious or worried about their future come across as a big turn-off. Take it slow on the first meeting, let him know that you are looking for a relationship, but wait for at least 5 to 6 weeks before sharing your future vision with him.

Interview Him

Remember that this is a date and not an interview. Take it slow and easy, and try to enjoy each and every minute you spend together. Even if you've already started liking him, take one step at a time. Don't ask too many questions, and stay away from private affairs, as it is a first date. Also, don't rate him according to every answer he gives. This can be highly irritable, and can lower the chances of a second meeting.

A few other things to remember are - don't put on too much makeup, indulge in clear communication, avoid behaving extra dainty, and single-word responses are a big turn-off, but that also does not mean that you chatter away to glory.

Remember, overdoing anything is the most visible sign of desperation. Also, avoid discussing your academic and professional achievements; he needs to know and understand you as a person, and not how hard you've tried to be successful at work. Try to relax and take it easy, after all, it is only the first date, and hopefully, there are many more to come.

CHAPTER 3- WHY DO MEN GET BORED IN RELATIONSHIPS

Do men get bored in relationships? Of course, they do. Anyone would, given the decision is made after rational thinking. Everybody, at least once in their lives, comes to a fork in their lives where they seem to require something more than a girlfriend or boyfriend, wife or husband. Relationships lose the excitement and charm it had in the beginning, and nothing seems to work out like it used to. Before, even the slightest touch from her fingers would attract you to her. The sweet smell emitting from her flowing locks mesmerized you beyond belief. And the passion in your kisses were too hot for you to handle. But these days, that intense connection and the need to be with her every single second has somehow disappeared. How can someone go from being obsessively involved with someone, waking up the next day and finding the relationship plain boring? No guy would just decide to lose interest in the girl he's with. What can be the reason behind this detachment?

Many a time, whenever something goes wrong in a relationship, both partners try to find reasons behind getting distant from one another. Every relationship has its own ups and downs where partners have to face challenges; hearts get broken, trust is shattered, and ill words are exchanged. Which is why, for every bump in the road, there is a valid reason behind it. So what can be the reason for a guy to become bored with his own girlfriend? Why do men get bored when in certain relationships? Are there any concrete reasons or just irrational and immature thinking is at play? Let's find out.

Why Do Men Run Away from Women?

It's not women (girlfriends or wives) they get bored of. What is missing in their lives is the feeling of excitement, spontaneity, thrill, passion, and perhaps romance. Some men thrive over the constant need to find something new that will satisfy them emotionally and physically. In this case, from their current and/or future partners. When all these things run their course, the exhilaration fizzles down. In the following section, there are few common instances/reasons, which can lead to lack of interest in a relationship for a guy.

He said - She was too easy to have. I need a challenge from a girl...

Some guys like girls who are hard to get. I guess it's some kind of notion they have in their minds that hard-to-get girls are much more exciting to be with. Whether this thinking is true or false, if a guy has such thoughts brewing in his mind, it could lead to dissatisfaction and boredom in any relationship.

He said - I cannot take her nagging at me all the time...

All men like to stay away from women who have the tendency to nag alot. In the beginning of the relationship, some women try to show their outgoing, carefree nature. However, if they incline towards being a controlling person, soon they end up expressing it out loud. The problem arises from frustration, it moves on to irritation, and then it quickly turns into wanting to be as far away from the person as possible.

He said - She doesn't want to be my girlfriend. She wants to be my WIFE...

I'll admit it. Most women think of marriage and babies after first few dates with a guy. This can lead a couple towards serious issues. I'm not trying to say that guys don't think about marriage, but they take their time in coming at this phase in their lives. Whether it's a man or a woman, marriage or any other serious commitment can't be forced upon them.

He said - Making love to her isn't as exciting as it used to be...

This is one of those reasons where every couple can have their own set of issues. What I mean to say here is that each individual has his/her own physical needs and it becomes important for them to fulfill those needs. Discontent and frustration can loom over any couple if these needs aren't met.

He said - I need my space and I need it right now...

Getting intimate and too serious in a relationship can be bad for anyone. It's natural when you feel that you wish to be with the one you love all the time, but distance is also crucial. Giving each other space so that you can miss the other person is the key to wanting to be with them. If you keep eating a particular ice cream flavor all the time and it's accessible to you 24/7, would you be interested in eating it the next time?

He said - She won't let me have my own life and friends...

This sort of overlaps with "I want my own space" reason. Giving a man (and woman) his own space and having your own personal, separate life is healthy for any couple. When a man sees that a woman doesn't re□uire anyone to take care of her all the time, they develop a sense of respect for her. This respect is very important for a woman as the feeling also turns into intrigue and wanting to be with her even more.

There are times when some of these reasons take shape into a man cheating on his girlfriend. The key here is to spice up your love life and actually enjoy the time the two of you share with one another. Changing either one of you won't do anyone any good. Be yourselves, keep all the cards on the table, and then decide whether the relationship is worth pursuing or not.

How well do you know your boyfriend?

He makes you feel wanted, special, loved, cared for and wipes away your every tear. He becomes your world and makes your fantasies of fairly tale romances come true. He will be there for you when hope's let you down, and despair, your erstwhile enemy has resurfaced. His will listen to your every complain, even when they are in vain. His insurmountable patience will calm your bouts of anger and make you fall in love with him all over again.

However, your boyfriend will lock away his darkest fears and protect them with an armed guards. Knowing his deepest emotions and his truest feelings is a Herculean task, as his secretive nature keeps his real self tucked away in an unreachable corner of his mind. So here's taking a look at five patterns of behaving that are ways to convey what they want to say.

We're Protective

The protective nature of men is misunderstood as extreme possessiveness. Smothering dos and don'ts stem from underlying fear that something might harm you. Those constant phone calls and text messages asking you, where you are, who you are with, and what you are doing are only because he wants to know that you are safe. At times, this behavior may intrude your space too. However, you need to understand where it comes from and assure him that you are old enough to take care of yourself.

He Needs to Talk

Men take time to let out their feelings. Additionally, they will never clearly state what they feel and what are the reasons for it. A guy will use hypothetical situations to convey his feelings. They do this, for they fear what trouble would an emotional spill cause. Get to know his friends better and allow him to befriend your friends. Even if he talks seem incoherent and incomplete, allow him to open up at his pace. If you rush, it may shut him up. Be supportive in your tone, to assure him that you'll always be there. The moment you draw a judgment, he will enter his shell which will make knowing him even more difficult.

Don't Pull Away

We women love playing the chase game. We love being chased. We enjoy the attention and the moment it stops, we feel a certain monotony creep in. So, many of us lve the whole coming-in-and-going-away game. In the initial stage, he may chase you keeping the playful charm alive. However, if you keep pulling away from him more than what should be done, he might start going away. This will not only lead to an emotional rift, but also cause a physical distance. When the game is to be played from the other end, it takes a nasty turn which could have a dead-end. So be careful of this tug-of-war. He may never tell you that he doesn't like the game or the distance, but his actions will speak louder than words.

Like His Friends ...Not Love

Yes, he will like you to be a part of his social circle and share a good rapport with his friends. But, if you ditch him, so that you can be with his friend(s) the relationship is sure to get sour. A man will never tell you not to be with his friends, because his camaraderie with them goes back a long way. So make sure you do not reciprocate to the love and affection his friends shower on you. Make a fine distinction between a platonic relationship and a romantic one.

Fear of Losing You

Even if this secret remains guarded life, the truth is that a man fears losing his women. Men are afraid of being heartbroken. This is the reason why he will go out of the way to do things for you. The fear of losing, also refrains men from confessing they love someone or resort to being a commitment phobia. In reality, men spend more time in thinking about losing their women, than actually being in love with them.

These behavioral patterns stem from underlying insecurities or fears, that most boyfriends guard. Thus, knowing them well, stops at knowing them well enough. Random fun ⬜uestions may give you answers to his favorite color, his favorite song, his favorite book and so forth. However, delving deeper into his behavior and being an active listener will help you know your boyfriend better.

Am i in love with him?

I can see him, even though he is absent,
I can feel him, although he is elsewhere,
I can hear him even when he is silent,
Is this love?
And there are thousands more thoughts alike, storming your mind just to assure that you are actually in love with him. A sweet shyness fills you when he is around and you wait

impatiently for him to speak up first. The smell of his perfume lingering in your senses after he has walked beside you. The nervousness in your eyes when you get caught observing him secretly. The restlessness in you when he is not around and the eagerness to meet him one more time drives you crazy. In a state of ecstasy, you ask yourself if you are in love with him? Well, these signs are □uite evident when you are truly in love and everything around you seems beautiful.

Your happiness multiplies when you observe him exhibiting the same behavior towards you. Eventually the expectations of both turn out to be true. You can confirm this better if you take up the love □uiz in the following segment. The □uestions are representations of the thoughts present in your mind while being in love. If your answers are 'yes', just exclaim in joy, 'I love him'.

Love Quiz

These apprehension of being truly in love or infatuation is making you confused. There are certain specific signs of falling in love, which help you to know whether you love him truly or not. We explain you over here.

Signs that you love him

You wishes to talk to him all the time.

His presence gives you joy and his absence makes you upset.

Facing him makes you a bit shaky.

You try to get noticed by him.

You wait for him to talk to you.

You dress up well when he is around.

You get impatient when you do not find him.

You show concern if he is upset.

You feel compelled to call him 'without' any reason (or text him).

You wait for his call anxiously (check your mobile repeatedly if he has pinged).

You see him first after waking up from sleep (hypothetically).

You includes him in your prayers (if you trust God).

The feelings for him

You feels that he is the world for you.

You are ready to accept him as your life partner.

You will be with him through thick and thin.

Your love is pure and selfless.

You respect him as well.

You feel jealous if he is close to some other girl.

You are ready to support him throughout life.

Things that you expect from him

You want him to be equally committed.

You want him to support you always.

You want him to love you truly.

You want him to respect you.

You want him to understand your sentiments and emotions.

Thoughts that make a difference

"If I could dream at all, it would be about you. And I'm not ashamed of it" ~ Stephenie Meyer

You feel a chill inside your spine when he touches you (a simple handshake!).

You have a secret desire to hug him.

You wait for him to plant the first kiss.

Think of the intimate moments entire day (smiles!).

Wait for him to touch you again (hold hands!)

You have a suppressed desire to love him.

You shall reciprocate to his desires without hesitation.

Test yourself...

If 80% of your answers revolve only around him, then you have simply fallen for him. Interesting? Well, take up the test.

How much do you love his personality

Okay

Improvement needed

Alot...

How do you feel in his company

Extremely happy

Better with friends

Boring and uncomfortable after a while

What do you do immediately after rising from bed

Check your phone to see if you have missed his call/text

You don't have time to check your phone

You do not respond even if he has called you

How do you feel after a misunderstanding

You do not care

You are too egoistic to patch up

You are hurt and want to patch up

How do you feel when you do not meet/contact each other

You don't really think much

Let him approach first

You miss him terribly and call up

I hope after testing yourself you are now convinced that you actually love him or not. You are a happy soul now and is living with the thought that 'love just happened, only if I could tell him at once.' Henceforth, you are waiting for him to disclose his feelings to you. Let your wait bear fruits soon! The feeling of being in love is just synonymous to Charles Morgan's quote, "there is no surprise more magical than the surprise of being loved."

NOTE: The □uiz was based on assumption that he has the same feelings for you.

Once you have committed yourself to your partner, there shouldn't be any □ualms in your mind. Welcome the joy of being in love and have happy days ahead.

Signs that shows he is not interested in you

Oh, that beautiful feeling when you really like someone! Just thinking about him makes butterflies flutter in your stomach; you re-read his one text message twenty times; those stolen glances; making excuses to talk to him, to see him. Often, girls tend to go that extra mile for a guy they have feelings for. From dressing up, to noticing small things about him and keeping them in mind, or doing stuff to make him happy, they try it all. How can I say for sure? Been there, done that. So have you? And still find yourself staring at the phone, waiting for him to call? You feel like he is not making enough effort to get to know you, or isn't appreciating what you do for him? Well, then let's face it girl! You need the man to be e☐ually interested in you to have a healthy relationship. Here are some signs that will help you understand whether the guy is probably interested in you or not. So brace yourself and read these to decide if you're heading down the wrong path.

Maybe He's Just Not That Into You

Gigi:Maybe his grandma died or maybe he lost my number or is out of town or got hit by a cab.

Alex: Or maybe he is not interested in seeing you again.

These lines are from the movie 'He's Just Not That Into You', which is actually based on the book by the same name, by Greg Behrendt and Liz Tuccillo, dealing with relationships and how women often misinterpret their romantic interest's actions and words. Decoding a guy's behavior is ideally no rocket science, and his actions usually speak volume

I'm Busy. Umm. With My PlayStation.

When you like someone, ideally, you want to spend all the possible free time together. But in your case, you are the one always making plans, and all he does is make excuses to not show up... not quite ideal, right? Once, twice, a guy can surely not be busy just about every time you talk about getting together. If he really likes you, a guy should be thrilled that you want to spend time with him, as it will give you both a chance to get to know each other better. However, if after repeated attempts from your end, he still does not seem to be reciprocating the enthusiasm to see you, he's just not worth it, bab

My Phone's Battery Died. Yeah Right!

When he is more into his phone than you

So you guys have exchanged numbers already? Good news. He takes hours to reply and probably days to call back? Not-so-good news. You might say, maybe he's busy with something. I say, it's not about being busy, it's about priorities.

If the only time he calls you is to return your calls, and you are the only one initiating conversation, be alarmed. Here's what you can do, try not getting in touch with him for few days, and see what happens. If he cares, he'll definitely wonder what's up with you and try to get in touch. And if not, just too bad for him.

You're My Nicest Girl 'Space' Friend.

When he is ignoring you

Damn that space between a girlfriend and a girl friend! I don't even need to talk about how annoying it is when your crush keeps referring to you as a very good friend. It's almost like he is constantly reminding himself and you that there is nothing more between you guys.

If he says he values the friendship too much etcetera etcetera, you have to stop and reconsider the situation, my friend. If he likes you, he will want to be with you, and more than just as friends. And if he cannot see you as his special someone, you've heard of the existence of other fish in the pond, the much better ones, right?

Is That Your Friend? She's Hot.

Whether they are single or committed, men check out other women, and that's a well-established fact. But when a guy is really into you, ignoring his occasional glances in other directions, he has his eyes exclusively on you.

If he tells you about his other female friends, great! It goes to show that he wants you to know about him and his personal life. But if he constantly looks at other women and talks openly about dating someone else, it's ꠸uite a clear sign that he is not going to be the one bringing you flowers and gifts to profess his love.

Oh, It's Your Birthday Today?

When he looks disinterested in your talks

You know his birthday, number, schedule, in addition to most of his hangouts and even favorite foods. And how do you think he would score on a ⬜uiz about you? Agreed, men are known to be not-so-great with birthdays and anniversaries, but when you really like someone, you want to know everything there is to know about that person. How can a guy be interested in you if he is not interested in getting to know you better?

Even basic things like asking about how your day was or what you did that evening, show that he cares. And if he isn't making an effort with small gestures like these, then maybe it's time to move on, and be with someone who genuinely cares.

Shhh. I'll Keep You My Secret.

When he doesn't want to sort out issues between the two of you

You like him so much that you cannot seem to stop talking about just how amazing he is, and how you cannot wait to see him. All your friends know everything there is to know about him, and have heard of every text message or interaction between the two of you, and are so eager to meet him. But every time you suggest that he comes and chills with your friends and you, he seems to have something else that needs to be done.

Sure enough, you have heard of his friends and what he did with them over the weekend, but have you ever met any of them? No? When you offer to go along and watch the games with him and his buddies, does he give you vague reasons and avoid? That should be your red light on the trouble meter. If you're the one, a guy will not miss a chance to show you off, and if you're not the one, he will, well, just play hide and seek.

Gentleman? Not Quite.

Chivalry in a man is □uite a turn-on for most women, and it just goes to show that he respects you. You are a beautiful, independent woman; but that does not have to stop him from at least offering to pay when you go out. Heard of the age-old cliché, if a guy likes you, he will make fun of you? Yeah, this one's true. But there is a difference between making light fun of you and saying something mean or offensive. Ignorance is another strong sign that a guy may not be quite into a girl.

To share a romantic bond, it is important for two people to respect each other's values and ideas. If this is not really the case with you and him, forget him, honey! Make efforts for someone who loves you and respects you for who you are.

These are some signs that may probably help you to get a better picture of where you stand when it comes to a romantic thing between you and the guy. If he isn't doing any of the above, then you've just got to give things some time. If some of these signs relate to his attitude, well, then it's time to focus on the other fish. And always remember what Marilyn Monroe said, "A wise girl kisses, but doesn't love, listens but doesn't believe, and leaves before she is left".

Qualities that men look for in every woman

Uncountable times, we have heard women stand up in unison and say, "Men will always be men, we know what they want." If only they knew what we really want! Culturally and socially, men have been stereotyped to be 'female hunters' or precisely, 'sexual predators'. While men fail to get the slightest idea of what women think, they themselves are no less complex and puzzling.

What Men Like in a Relationship

It seems that the idiosyncrasies of both genders is a necessity for their peaceful coexistence. All those women who have been patiently waiting to know 'what men like in a woman', read further to discover their minds. This article shall honestly tell you about what men really want. (Believe us! We men don't lie always.)

Physical Intimacy

You needn't frown, ladies! By physical intimacy, it frankly means kisses, hugs, and ... sex. At times, we are obsessed with sex and sports (may be the genes are constituted such), and we may wish you'd look like the next Bond girl! However, this doesn't mean we end up here. There is a lot more to men than what meets the eye. We do honestly wish to take sometime and know our women. And, let's not just pretend that it is only men who like sexually active partners. Even women do want it, though they may not be so vocal about it (or are they?).

We do cross the boundaries of lust, and we do have a craving to be really special for our special someone. Sharing and exploring finer dimensions of our girl's personality, is what we really want to do. Physical bonding is just one of the many desires of men. We look for it, but we don't run after it. We are much more deeper than the realms of that 'physical' word. There are various other reasons why men like women. Honestly, you have to believe us!

Attractiveness

Before you grossly misjudge attractiveness to just one dimension of physical beauty, you ought to be aware that attractiveness is quite a relative concept, and can have different meanings for every man. While we don't deny that a nicely chiseled, slim, and well-rounded figure, long hair, beautiful eyes, and stunning smiles can sweep us off our feet, those are not the only traits that can drive us crazy.

A woman's elegance and confidence are often more important criteria for most men. A dressing sense that exudes sensuousness in a positive manner, has a huge appeal for us. More than being a blond, we want women to look beautiful in their own comfort zone. We love it if you dress up for us. Attractiveness can spring from the way you talk, from your sense of humor, behavior, and expressive prowess. We find a show-off nature in a woman extremely annoying. Being yourself is always the safest path for both, men and women, especially in a healthy relationships.

Some of the obvious things men love about women are not difficult to comprehend. A brightly lit face, with the tinge of a sweet smile, hair falling down to the shoulders, and few enigmatic glances can leave us bewitched. We don't like dumb women, and we appreciate a soft and sweet voice, instead of shrill, loud-mouthed females. We find you attractive when you are adventurous, and even if you are a prankster. We find attractiveness in those females around whom we feel comfortable. We don't expect you to be perfect a 10; a little less is never a problem. After all, nobody is perfect.

No Nagging and No Bitching

Girls, we know that bitching is an integral part of your nature. Men, however, hate it. Seriously, we can never tolerate it. It sometimes goes beyond our logic to give some of our expert comments on your bitching topic(s), and hence, we remain silent, nodding our heads.

You can talk to your girlfriends, but when you come to us, don't expend your energy again on the same topic. We can talk about soccer or ice hockey, but we can hardly digest serious bitching. Don't think of us as insensitive beings; we are always ready to listen to you on any matter. Men admire women who don't bitch to them. Aren't there more beautiful topics to talk about?

Nagging is another repelling factor for men. Although we're used to nagging by our mothers, we never want it to be done by you. Give us our due space and freedom! We will come back to you, at the end of the day. We love to be listened to, and cared for. When we're around you, we really don't get your gossips and discussions.

Trust, Love, and Care

Men appreciate sweet gestures that shower love upon them. We love it when you slowly whisper, "I love you, honey", in our ears. You need to pamper us at least once in a while. Being treated like a kid sometimes does give us some sense of assurance and much-needed love. When you cook for us, we feel more than happy. We love when you shop for us, and when you reply to our calls and texts, be it in the midnight or wee hours of the morning. We enjoy your surprises and crackling laughter.

No matter how free we act, deep down in our hearts, we do need a sense of security. At some stage, when our testosterone is balanced and wisdom takes over our recklessness, we do wish to be in a serious relationship. The feeling of security in a relationship does matter to us, and we want a woman who can build our trust, and make us believe that we can win the world (with some doses of ego feeding).

Occasional pampering helps us to make the seemingly impossible, possible. Sometimes, we get annoyed when you try to cut through our ego, and if you say we can't do a certain thing. Someone who can accept a certain part of our craziness, and love us unconditionally (we do respond back with the same) is what we admire in women.

Mutual trust and understanding is the biggest need of every man who wishes to be in a committed relationship. So, in essence, we seek understanding partners who can shower us with abundant love, and we feel that only an understanding woman can give us that.

Chamber of Secrets

Often, women are like angels (something for you ladies to feel proud about). As a popular saying goes, "A woman can either make or break a man." Certainly, they have something magical, some 'chamber of secrets', that can channelize a man's energies from female-hunting or recklessness to a specific path. Not surprisingly, men often say that their wife or girlfriend is the best thing that has happened to them.

We agree that women make a significant contribution in our success, in our professional as well as personal lives. We may not show that we wish to be guided and possessed, but in our minds, we feel that belonging to someone is an amazing feeling. A partner to share our deepest desires, joys, and pleasures is what guys need.

No Infiltrators

Call it a male ego, but we don't like you talking too much about your ex, or for that matter, any other guy. Many women will define it to be a manifestation of the male ego, jealousy, or even insecurity. The matter of fact is that we hate it. We don't like talking too much about your past, so don't assume that we are intolerant or insensitive. We are ready to listen to you. In fact, we love listening to you.

Even women won't accept infidelity or any extramarital affairs. So, you've got to give it to us as well. Bonding and trust from a woman's side is the most important quality that we look for. Hence, when someone tries to infiltrate the our-heart-zone-territory, we can, at times, be violent and break their head.

Relationships and marriage are a process of growing up with your partner. Besides growing old, one has to grow up with the partner, at every level. When a man really likes a woman, he experiences a different realm altogether. In this world, things move beyond the physical (sounds archaic, but it's the ultimate truth), and his energies transcend 'love' to be more than a physical or emotional experience. However, this stage comes to different men at different ages. For some men, the happy realization, that his partner has been the best gift ever, comes late. For some lucky few, it comes early.

Those men get a sense of personal and spiritual satisfaction. Once attained and felt, this drives them from being egoistical and tough, to acting selflessly for their love. Unconditional love, that is what is experienced, surpassing all human limitations. At such a stage, they truly feel what Antoine de Saint-Exupéry has beautifully expressed, "Love does not consist in gazing at each other, but in looking together in the same direction."

Last but not the least, there is no fixed formula or standard, that can read a man's mind and tell his thoughts about a lady. Depending on individual preferences, different men may like different attributes in women. So ladies, you need not worry! Just like you, we too are very confused souls. Who knows? The very next man you encounter could be exactly the opposite of what's written here.

CHAPTER 4- GETTING HIM COMMIT TO YOU

You've been with a man for some time now, you talk about the future alot and everything seems to be great except he still hasn't popped the question and you are left wondering why. You analyze every aspect of your life together- you both are financially stable, you love each other to death but he never said he wants to marry you. And then you are left clueless on how to get him commit to marriage. Maybe it's time for you to assess yourself and not just your relationship.

One of the most important things in a successful relationship is when you know how to love yourself. Ask yourself this question- would you marry YOU? Are you happy with yourself? If the answer is NO then don't expect others will be. If you are always whining about your job or the extra 5 lbs. you just can't lose, do you think somebody would want to be around that for the rest of their life? Be more positive and love yourself more. Be that kind of person that your partner wants to spend the rest of his life with.

Another mistake that most women make is that they jump the gun and they choose to live in their own fantasy world. Before you start looking at wedding dresses or wedding venues, wait until your man actually pops the □uestion. Don't talk about getting married or how many kids you want. That would just turn him off and do the exact opposite of what you have in mind. Don't ever take him window shopping for engagement rings because that spells desperation. The only time you should talk about getting married is when your boyfriend brings it up.

You also don't need to scare your boyfriend by telling him that once you get married and have a child, you are going to quit your job and just be a stay-at-home mom. Women are notorious for making plans way in advance. We meet a guy we like and we're already picturing ourselves wearing a white gown and imagine how it feels like waking up next to him for the rest of our lives. What else is wrong with telling a guy that you'll be jobless after you get married? He will probably think that you just want to marry him to secure your future and you just want somebody to sponsor the lifestyle that you want.

If you truly want a guy to ask your hand in marriage, you have to show him that you are independent and self-sufficient. Unless the man suggests it and unless there's an absolute need for you to quit your job, please keep your job. You don't want your man to think that you are going to depend on him for the rest of your lives together.

Instead of acting desperate on getting married or playing hopeless in the waiting game, give your man the impression that you are not afraid to remove yourself from a relationship that is going absolutely nowhere. Love is never enough to stay in a relationship. You have the right to know if you are waiting for nothing. Make him feel that you cannot keep investing in a relationship that will end up being stagnant. Remember that you are not someone whom he can string along until a more suitable woman comes along for him to marry. If it's obvious that he is dragging it for as long as he can then tell him that you would like to start seeing other people. Avoid being overly dramatic so he'll know you mean business and that is if you want to be successful on how to get him to commit to marriage. Gather enough courage and don't be afraid to lose him. Better do this now than regret it 5 years later and he still hasn't proposed.

How to show him you care

He'll see you do stuff for him and appreciate it, but won't really understand the importance of that care until it is shown to him. Then there are those guys who are so busy with their lives, that this emotions just don't reach them the way they should. Then there are those who take a step ahead and actually tell you that you don't care enough. Ouch, that might hurt? Guys don't understand feelings until they are put right there, all out on the table, up for a careful observation. They just don't function that way. You are now going to find out some of the best ways to show your boyfriend you care.

Tips

Tell Him You Do

Yes, it's as simple as that. Tell him you care for him in one of the sweetest ways possible and that he can tell you if he needs something. Guys like this attitude. It's simple and they understand it better. They know they can rely on you and that's how they like it. Find some cute ☐uotes for him, that will help you convey the message. Tell him how it troubles you to not know if he's okay or not. You can also say this over a phone call, leave notes around the house, send him text messages to say so, or have a heart-to-heart conversation about it.

Remind Him of Stuff

One of the best ways to show your boyfriend you care is to remind him of stuff that he tends to forget. Paying his bills, keeping his habits in check, and other things he needs to get done in time are some of the things we women take care of. You won't have to try hard to find these, as guys usually tend to forget quite a lot. Sometimes I feel they forget it, only because we can remind them about it. Tell him to have his meals on time and make sure he does. Actions speak louder than words, don't they?

Take Some Efforts

You needs to take some efforts so that he realizes how much you care for him. If you guys are in the same town, you can cook his favorite meals from time to time. If he stays alone, you can help him with the grocery shopping and the maintenance of the home. You can make sure his place is tidy and clean enough for him to live in.

Perfectly Pamper Him

One of the best ways to show your boyfriend you care is by pampering him perfectly. If he has alot to complain, you should be listening to him, no matter how boring it might get. If he has alot of issues, listen to them all. Give him that head massage once in a while and cook for him often. Buy him small gifts even though there isn't an occasion that demands it.

Show Him the Difference

Sometimes, the best way to show something is by showing how it doesn't exist somewhere else. This will indirectly apply that is exists here. Similarly, show your boyfriend how other girls don't care for their boyfriends and how this irritates you. Tell him how much you think it is necessary for partners in a relationship to care for each other. Work done!

With the help of these tips, you will surely be able to tell your boyfriend that you care for him. It is very necessary that you convey such things to him, to bring out the positive aspects in your relationship. He will not only appreciate the care you unconditionally offer, but will also respect you for it. I hope showing him this care brings in more happiness in your relationship.

How to make him want you more

Tips

Take Care of Him

Guys love to be pampered and taken care of; they may not show this but they do. Pamper him. Cook for him, shop for him, surprise him, and listen to him. However, don't go overboard with it. Don't ask him too many ⬜uestions. All you need to do is actively take interest in what's been up with him.

Look Good for Him

There is nothing more a man likes than a woman who tries to impress him. Who would not like a woman that dresses up well and is never not presentable? Want to go one step further? Get yourself a makeover!

Keep Him Happy

Do things that make him happy. Cook his favorite food, wear his favorite color, take him to dine at his favorite restaurant ... let your world revolve around him. Let him know, you know what he likes. Don't ask for anything in return and don't even tell him that you are doing all this for him. Let him realize that on his own and he'll treasure you more than before.

Retain Your Individuality

Don't cling to him all the time. You have to learn the art of being one and yet maintain your individuality. Don't make yourself one of his liabilities; be his asset. Guys love individualistic girls. See to it that you have a life of your own; don't smother him.

Be There for Him

Guys can't convey emotions easily. They find it difficult to express what they think or what they're going through. At such times, be there for him unconditionally. Let him know that he can always fall back on you. Try to be a girl he can come home to. You have to be a constant support for him during his tough times. Give him the courage to try harder when he fails. Show him your faith in him.

Be genuine with what you feel for him. Guys like girls who are sorted out and not emotionally complicated. This does not mean you stop communicating your emotional troubles, it means you stop letting them control your relationship.

How do men fall in love

We have been discussing and suggesting' number of ways to make a man fall in love with you. But they are all irrelevant if you do not have the basic understanding of how a man's brain works, vis-a-vis his interest in the opposite sex is concerned. Here is some interesting info on the different stages that men go through, when they fall in love.

Stage One: Physical Attraction

Unlike women, who look more for security, comfort, emotional connection with their prospective partners to have any feeling of intimacy, most men fall in love with a woman, just because of her good looks. Men's brains are naturally programmed to look at women from the point of view of prospects who will carry on their genes. So, they are always attracted to women who seem healthy (read: curvaceous), young, and energetic. In fact, many men are known to have fallen in love head over heels with a woman in the first meeting itself.

Stage Two: Mental Stimulation

Men are very visual creatures. They can be simultaneously physically attracted to lot of women. So what is it that will make a man fall in love with one particular woman? Well, it could be anything, sometimes as simple as how she laughs or talks, or how she is passionate about something. It could be her sense of humor or intelligence, whatever that distinguishes her from other women. Once he feels that a particular woman is fun to be with, has her own interests and life, and that he enjoys her company to a great extent, then it can be said that stage two of his falling in love, has arrived. In this stage, he finds her unique and special, may even consider dating exclusively, and also protects her from the advances made by other men towards "his" woman.

Stage Three: Emotional Connection

It is easier to identify that a man is in love, when he forms an emotional connection with a woman. In this stage, the man will start to see his future with the woman. He will have no problem declaring his love to her, and also to his friends and family. He will start thinking "we" instead of "me", and the same will translate into his actions.

To predict exactly when men fall in love or how is not that easy. A sure shot way to know it is when he starts missing your presence. There are lot of ways to make him fall in love with you such as showing him your sensitive side, giving him full freedom, respecting his opinions, having your own life away from the relationship, and making him a happier person by tickling his funny bone, every now and then. If you think that you are capable of doing all this, there is no way a man can resist your charms.

So going by that, being physically attractive, mentally alert, energetic, and full of life, are all the essential ingredients which a woman should possess to win a man's heart.

How to make him happy

Make Him Feel Important

Be honest and understanding with him. Make him feel as if he is the only guy in the world for you, by expressing your love for him. Buy him a small gift like a card saying how much you love him, or just make a late night phone call telling him that you just wanted to hear his voice, and the likes.

Give Him Space

Give him air to breathe, by not complaining when he stays out with his friends. Men also need their time with their friends, so, do not hassle your guy too much when he plans a boys night out once or twice a month. Don't be jealous and clingy, as these are two traits that men strongly dislike.

Keep Your Relationship Young

No matter how long you have been with your guy, you still need to flirt with him. It makes him feel wanted and important. Holding hands and exchanging playful remarks, helps keep your relationship playful and romantic.

Keep Your House Clean

Believe me, we men are disorganized but cleanliness is one thing that turns us on. We love that our room and our house is spot free, it automatically brightens up the mood and ensures that the next few hours are all going for the lady's praise.

Compliment Him

If you don't give your partner enough compliments start now. This is a very common misconception that only girls love compliments. Guys love hearing praises, tell him that you are lucky to have him. Put him on cloud 9 by admiring things that are important to him, like his bike, new haircut, or even his boxing gloves.

Cook His favorite Food

The saying, 'a way to man's heart is through his stomach', may sound old-fashioned, but it's 100% true. You don't have to be a expert in cooking just making him something small will make you the queen of his heart for centuries to come.

Be Truthful

Be truthful about your feelings and thoughts, as men are not supernatural creatures that can read minds. When it comes to a serious relationship, they expect their woman to be brutally honest with them. So, if you have any insecurities, or are feeling low, giving him an 'I am fine' answer will never help.

Support him in his ambition, as you are an important part of his life. Make small gestures, as they go a long way in strengthening and cementing a relationship. Always be there for him when he is low, as men are very emotional even if they do not show it.

CHAPTER 5- LOVE ADVICE FOR YOUNG GIRLS

Young girls can often be a tad too hasty in the matters of the heart. They often over-dramatize the happenings in their lives, and so if relationships are not handled properly, they may leave permanent scars on their minds. Giving them sugesstions is a little tricky and complicated, with the adviser constantly treading on eggshells. So if you are a young lady, treading down newly blooming love paths, here's some relationship advice for girls that should help you out.

Prere□uisites

No advice can begin without a note on finding out whether you are emotionally capable of handling a relation. The trick of a successful relationship lies in being emotionally mature and independent. Do not develop an obsession with finding Mr. Right. You're still young and you have a long way to go with a lot of things to learn. The idea is to keep a neutral mind, for when you're not looking is when you're most likely to find him. Know what you want, because if you're the one confused, how can your partner not be? Only if you have set some credentials that you're looking for in your man, will you know if you've met the right one. Varying your demands will lead you to lose 'good men' (and yes the two can be used together in one phrase). Most of the time things go wrong, not because the guy is wrong, but because you've changed your criteria. Last, but not the least, if you do have a picture of what you want in a man, don't hold on to it like the Gospel. Be flexible, and you never know, maybe the guy you have is the perfect one for you, though he doesn't fit in with your initial criteria.

Lose The 'Adopt a Fella' Syndrome

Many young girls fall for bad boys who are lost causes. Such relations are disastrous. The problem with the female gender is that they take their nurturing abilities a bit too far. A hungry puppy, an injured bird, or an unfortunate guy, all have a capacity to pull at a girl's heartstrings. The more you think that they need you, the more you'll get sucked into a vicious world of parasitic bonds. You do not need a clinging creeper to support, you need a man to laugh with, cry with, and love. This is not the man girl! Drop him, and drop him fast. Let them sort out their own problems, while you get back to your search of Mr. Right again.

Be Alert to the Signs

There are many subtle and not-so-subtle signs that a guy can give away when near a woman, that state his level of interest in you. Study body language, and you'll soon learn to discern the genuine from the pretense. Learn the signals, and you can stop potentially heartbreaking attachment. Don't cut him slack just because you like him. If you see signs that he is just playing you, don't turn a blind eye towards it (girls do have this tendency to keep a man on a pedestal, and make excuses to keep him there). It is important that while you keep an eye open to look for his signs and signals, don't confuse him with conflicting ones from you. The key advice for girls who have a crush on someone is to give it a fair shot and not color the relationship with preconceived notions of what should and should not be. And yes, don't cling (easier said than done). Let him have a life apart from you, and let him know that you have one too. No one likes constricting relations, and so, make sure that you give each other enough breathing space.

Be an E☐ual

Unless you have a hidden desire to be a common hausfrau who bends to his wishes at every opportunity, you need to carry yourself well in the initial stages of courtship. Talk to him as an e☐ual. There is a thin line between assertive and affirmative. Make sure that you maintain it. Be more than a wallflower, and make sure it is visible in everything you do. The very minute you let a man think that he can erase your voice with his, it will be very difficult to convince him otherwise. It is a genetic flaw with men, they tend to take one's offs as something that can happen all the time. So, unless you wish to be pushed around, be yourself when you meet him (and when you're yourself make sure you tell him so), and try not to be too subservient (and if you are, don't make it a habit).

Leave Behind the Sentimental Mumbo Jumbo

Most females have a habit of considering that their guys are entirely too good for them. That stinks of something I call emotional crap. He is most definitely not too good for you, for you can't see how very special you are. Everyone is special in their own way. Another thing, don't go looking for that (impossible) man of your dreams. Mostly, the guy you end up with, eventually becomes your prince charming anyway. And then, all your fairy tales will be with him as the main lead. Be a little realistic, and know that whoever you end up with, will be the one made for you, and you do not need to go out looking for him.

Miscellaneous Advice

Here are some pointers of what you should and should not do when in the early stages of a relation:

There's just one essential rule, know what you want, and go after it with all your might.

Don't get so involved that you lose your identity. Never change yourself for a man.

Get a dose of reality, and listen to what your friends have to say. Sometimes, their opinions are more unbiased than yours, when you're already wearing rose-tinted glasses.

Absolutely do not make excuses for your guy. Some things never change, so if he's chronically violent or jealous, run far away from this relation. Abuse should not be tolerated at any stage.

If your relationship fails, and you end up with a breakup on your hands, don't despair. Firstly, don't ever take it personally. Secondly, losing him won't be the end of your world. No one dies of heartbreak, and as of today, it is not listed anywhere as a fatal illness.

How to be a good girlfriend

Being a good and caring girlfriend is a nice way of letting your boyfriend know, how lucky he is to have you. You don't have to go out of your way to be 'good', just to please your boyfriend. You already have it in you, that is why your boyfriend chose you in the first place. You just have to express what you genuinely feel about your boyfriend. Yet, if you feel like going that extra mile for pleasing him, you can indeed go through these tips on how to be a good girlfriend, presented in this book.

Give Him Space - Don't Nag

Most girls are so overwhelmed with the feeling of having a boyfriend that they tend to cut themselves off from the rest of the world and expect their boyfriends to do the same. However, there is a difference in the way men and women look at a relationship. Women tend to devote all of their time to their new relationship, while men only think of it as a addition to their existing ones. However, that does not mean that your boyfriend does not want to spend time with you, but he sure needs his own space. Let your boyfriend spend time with his friends and family if he really wants to. Don't nag all the time, because nagging is something men really hate. After all, what's the use of having a boyfriend by your side all the time, when his mind   is   somewhere   else?

Be Independent

Men really like women who are independent and capable of taking care of their lives. Calling your boyfriend at the slightest sign of trouble is definitely not a good idea. In the initial stages of a relationship, your boyfriend may like it when you turn to him for help, for every petty reason, however he may gets irritated, if you make it a habit. Instead, show him that you can look after yourself and can handle problems without having to rely on him. It is best if you make yourself financially independent as well. Not only will it help you to support yourself but it will also garner your boyfriend's respect and appreciation.

Share His Interests

Sharing his interests and participating in his favorite activities is a nice way of showing your boyfriend, that you are ready to go that extra mile to make the relationship work. Obviously, nobody expects you to enjoy his activities as much as he does, but your willingness to share his interest will make your boyfriend very happy. Sacrificing a romantic flick for a football match, once a while, can help you build a healthy relationship, without you knowing it.

Be Honest

Be honest to yourself and your boyfriend but do not expect it in return. You can be honest about your life, your past relationships, your ex-boyfriend etc., but it is unfair to expect the same from him. He may have his own reasons for not divulging details of his past, so respect his feelings. However, you can always communicate your feelings and expectations. Being honest about your expectations from the relationship will help both of you to understand where your relationship stands.

Don't Be Overtly Possessive

Although, over-possessiveness is usually associated with guys, some girls just don't let go of their boyfriends and cling to them all the time. Beware girls, this attitude may make your guy claustrophobic and it won't be too long before he sees red. Don't confront him if some chick checks out your guy because it is not his fault. Instead, be happy that you are dating a guy, most girls would be desperate to be with. Similarly, don't hack his passwords and read his mails or text messages. Such behavior may make you look like a desperate person who feels insecure about her relationship.

Don't Be a Control Freak

Most girls try to get the control of the relationship by trying to change something about their boyfriends. Criticizing his looks, clothes, habits can really turn him off. Just as you would not want to change yourself for anyone, your boyfriend also loves himself the way he is. Always remember that you fell for him for what he is. If there is something unpleasant about him or his appearance, give him subtle hints, don't ever yell at him for that will make the matter worse.

Be Patient

Men do not believe in expressing their feelings the way women do, hence be patient if your boyfriend seems in a somber mood and refuses to talk to you. Do not frustrate him by asking too many ⬜uestions. Just leave him alone, he'll himself come back to you whenever he feels like talking about whatever was bothering him.

Don't Ask Awkward Questions

Women have this habit of asking a wrong question at a wrong time. Nothing infuriates a man more than a 'do you love me?' amidst a romantic sequence. Use your common sense ladies, would he be with you if he never loved you in the first place? Do not expect your boyfriend to profess his love for you, all the time. And for God's sake, refrain from asking him 'how much?' if he ever bothers to answer your first question.

Being a good girlfriend is really not that difficult if you let your guy get some life and learn to get some yourself. You may feel like you are sacrificing some things in the process of becoming a good girlfriend but remember these small sacrifices go a long way in consolidating your relationship. Finally, follow the above tips only if you think your boyfriend is worth it, else you know what to do!

Should I call him?

Maintaining a relationship is one of the toughest part, as it is not at all a bed of roses. There are many ups and downs; in fact, there are loads of downs and just a couple of ups! When starting a new relationship, many things are decided upon, but as the relationship proceeds, these vows turn out to be just meaningless words.

Some might feel this ⬚uestion is pointless, but these people have definitely not gone through the tumults of conscience that one faces when it comes up. The problem is not of just dialing a few numbers, but more about "why me". Every time this question erupts, there is an underlying stubborn wish that the other person should take the initiative. Everybody feels that it is the other person's responsibility to take the initiative, whether it be after a fight or after a date. Sometimes, it is the ego that does not allow the person to take the initiative, while sometimes it is self-esteem. If it is the ego, you need to curb it and if it is the self-esteem, you should not put your foot down. But how should one decide? Well, it depends on the situation, and some of the most common situations are given below.

Should I Call Him After a Breakup?

Dealing with a breakup is a Herculean task. There are a very few lucky people who have a smooth breakup, i.e., without any cursing, tears, and wounded hearts. Most of the time, the cause of breakup is not the situation or the person, but the words that were said in the heat of the moment, which actually should have never been uttered. These things can never be forgotten by the other person, which generally leads to a breakup.

After the moment is past, one often regrets the said words. First of all, think once again why the breakup happened, and try to keep the emotions out this time. What caused it? Why did you come to such a big decision? Keep your mind cool and think again of the things that hurt you or made you feel insulted in your relationship. If you think of giving a second chance, can you be sure that the other person won't make the same mistakes again? And most importantly, do you think you can forget everything that happened? If the answers to these questions are yes, you can call him. But if the answers are no, you should not make the mistake of calling. No doubt it will be difficult to stop yourself from contacting him after the anger settles down, but remember that the decision of separating has been taken for some concrete reason. It has ended because it was not going the way you had thought it would.

Should I Call Him After a Fight?

Conflicts is part and parcel of any relationship. The differences that hardly mattered at the start of the relationship become the cause of wars after a while. The things which are said and done during a fight generally vanish afterward. So, it may seem safe to call. But when we call to apologize, the same things which caused the fight are repeated and again lead to the blame game and another fight! So curb your impulses, and do not call for at least a few hours after the fight (the exact duration depends on the nature of the fight). Before calling him, think of all the possible answers that can come from his side. Remember only the negative responses that you can get. Practice to be calm even after the worst possible response, and when you think you are now foolproof to anger and curses, call him.

Should I Call Him After a Date?

This is one of the most common questions faced by modern girls. Before deciding to contact him, first think to yourself whether you really like that guy and would like to go again on a date with him. If the answer is yes, then wait. Even if you have fallen head over heels for him, do not call at least for 24 hours. Have some patience and see if he calls you. If he doesn't call even after 24 hours, you can make a call but do not even accidentally ask him why he didn't call. This question will only show your desperation and give him a winning edge. Talk about any random things for a few minutes and then casually ask him if he would like to catch up.

How to tell if a guy is serious about you

A woman's psyche is popularly labeled as inscrutable. However, a man's mind is equally difficult to understand, if not more or less. The element of seriousness in a relationship is a two way street. So, if you are thinking of taking your relationship to new level of commitment, you need to know whether he feels the same way about it. Being on the same page and moving alongside each other in terms of thoughts and sentiments is important for relationship to grow. But if you are unable to figure out what he is thinking, then you need get a little observant. Watching his actions will tell you more than what words can say.

He's a Man of his Word

How many times have you waited for his call, when he says 'I'll call you back'? If the answer is zero, then here's a sign that needs to be noted. If time is not a luxury in his life and yet he makes a effort to squeeze a call, just to say a hello, it's time you take the cue. He may talk incoherently about random things that don't matter much, or the conversation might be a brief one. But, how does it matter, as along as he sticks to his promise? It really doesn't. Calling you up fre□uently, returning your calls and sticking to his promises are the first signs that say he likes you. Now, the underlying reasons are; one, he wants to hear your voice and two, to gauge your interest in his activities. By tell you things about him, he is trying to make you a part of what he does and who he is.

No More Mind Games

When he says he'll be going out with his friends, he tells you who they are. He is comfortable with the idea of making you a part of his social circle and encourages you to get to know his friends better. There is no pretext involved in going out or phone conversations with someone else. If he is talking to his ex-girlfriend, he tells you so in absolute honesty. When a man is being so transparent about his life, it is a sign that the mind games are over and the relationship you share is no longer casual. It means more to him than any other lie. His effort to be honest and open, is a definite sign that says he wants to be with you.

He Wants To Know

Asking him some ⬜uestions such as 'what is your favorite book?' or 'what are your dreams and ambitions?' may not help you find out one's truest emotions and deepest feelings. But if he being an active listener (most men are not) to your rantings, complaints, conversations you make with him and late night phone calls, then he genuinely wants to get to know you better. He wants to know the person you were, before you met him. Even if every silly detail of your life seems interesting to him, then understand that he is trying to derive a meaning.

Your Opinion is Valued

We women like men who are decisive in nature, but we also like it when a man asks for an opinion. So, if he asks you to accompany him to buy clothes, it's only because he wants to know your opinion. If he asks you about your opinions while making big decisions such as picking a job, it shows that he values your thoughts and in more ways than one, your opinion has a certain influence on him.

Makes You Feel Special

If he makes sure that everyone around him knows that you are his steady girlfriend, then there is more to it than just dating. If his philandering ways have been replaced by faithfulness and fidelity, it is a sure shot sign that he's serious about you. The relationship you share is exclusive and above anyone's judgment. Also, if he has made it clear to his ex that he is with you, it's only because he wants show his commitment. This is a huge move and he sure deserves appreciation.

Men are a little secretive about their feelings. So, if he hasn't told you that he is serious about your relationship, then these are the signs that will tell you so. The fact that he is there for you always, despite the pressures of his job or anything else, is an indisputable notification of the fact that, you mean a lot to him. The answer lies in his behavior towards you. Watch him closely, and give him time to build a comfort zone, where he can be more open about the way he feels. Don't forget that a man's biggest fear is losing his woman. And it is this fear, that makes a man chose his words carefully.

CHAPTER 6- CONCLUSION

There's nothing ☐uite like the initial stages of attraction, is there? The stolen glances, the fluttery feelings, the unspoken signals that can leave your emotions skyrocketing one moment and nosediving the next; the secret playoff between two people on who will make the famous over-hyped "first" move. Now I'm all for the modern, liberated woman, but if you're looking for ways and means to ask a guy out, that's not really my forte. What I can do, however, is give you the ways and means to get a guy interested enough, and if your stars are in alignment, maybe ask you out.

When it comes to proposing, my views are more conventional with a modern tinge. I believe that you should help the guy, through hints and gestures, to let him know that you like him, but the rest is up to him. I know it sounds backward, old-fashioned - call it whatever you want - but isn't it way better to have a guy tongue-tied about asking you out? See what I mean? Men and relationships are subjects that have bewildered women from time immemorial. The subtle art of seduction needs some serious work, as does figuring out what to say to a guy you like, so that you don't sound like a complete dork. Take a look at some possible scenarios and dating tips.

Take Your Pick

Your approach depends on whether you are meeting your 'prince charming' in person or conversing through texting, so first figure out which way you wish to go.

In a Text

You know, of all the inventions that the modern world has foisted on us, I think texting ranks way up there with iPods and Swiss knives (is it a knife, is it a scissor, is it a toothpick, who can tell?). Why? Simply because it gives you the ability to plan what you say, and you can come out looking super smart, even though you've erased and rewritten seventeen times before you hit "send". How cool is that? And in a situation where all depends on sounding 'super cool', that's a serious advantage.

So, we're going to assume you're already on a text footing with this guy (very good work so far) and want to take it ahead from there. Since you have each other's phone numbers, I'm also going to assume that you know each other, if only as ac□uaintances - maybe you study together, work together, or just meet at a hobby class. What you say need not be seeped in emotion - in fact I'll go as far as to say that don't get even a hint of emotion to begin with. Keep it light, keep it friendly and keep it oh, so casual. If it's you that's starting the texting, start off with something that's vaguely common, not so much of a flirty text message - maybe a funny one-liner (but please not an obvious forward) or maybe something that happened at class. If you're up to it, skip a class and ask him if you could borrow some notes - a perfect conversation starter! Follow the one-minute rule; after reading his text, wait for one minute before replying. This helps in setting a casual atmosphere and you don't come across as jobless and "lifeless". More or less the same rules apply to an email - light and casual is the mantra, chant while you type.

In Person

The difficult thing is to behave in a manner that's not contrived; in a situation that is contrived. If you find yourself fre□uently tongue-tied, remember that it's better to seem □uiet than stupid, really. Loosen up a bit though - make a casual conversation, but draw the line at seeming perky and bubbly, if you're not, and vice-versa.

Figuring out a bunch of cool things to say to a guy and feeling flustered isn't really going to help. If you two get together, it should be on the basis of what you really are, so keep it real. Do some research on books, movies or music he might like, and bring them up in the conversation; that should help. If he likes you or finds you interesting, he's likely to keep it going himself, so don't seem too pushy, and as a rule, end the conversation, text marathon or email spree, with a breezy 'see you later' manner. That gives him a chance to get back to you himself.

Things to Get Close To

Here are few lines that will guide you on how your conversation with a guy should be:

Compliments

With a smile on your face and a little love in your tone, shower the guy with genuine and sometimes, may be exaggerated compliments. It's not only for boys, but everyone loves compliments. Slip them in the middle of the conversation subtly. Guys may not come across as the ones who are particular about their appearance, but they care about it as much as girls, so using lines like Trendy shoes!, I love your watch, or something more intimate like Your cologne smells nice! will do the trick.

Teasing

To spice up the chase, and to catch his attention, tease the guy a little. You can do this by pointing out a cheesy line used by him, or say "Oh! Did you think you won me over?". Do not go till the extent of continuously putting him down. The aim is to pull him few notches down and see how he will overdo himself to prove his worth. Guys are very competitive and they make it point to get even with you.

Hard-to-get Attitude

Remember that the thrill is in the chase; even a guy doesn't like a girl who is easy to get. So even if you are head over heals for this guy, let him work his way into your life. Here is one trick, you can use. If he asks you to meet him on Saturday, tell him that you are busy, but don't cancel the plan. Try postponing it to Sunday. This will project that he is important to you, but you also have a life of your own. Get him to tell you things about himself; do not ask directly.

Parting Words

The golden rule is "your conversation with the guy should be memorable for him", and no one remembers a boring conversation. So, the moment the conversation hits a downhill, make way for your parting words and leave. Before leaving, appreciate the time you have spent with him. You can use lines like "After long, I have had such a great time!, I didn't know how time flew! or if you are a little shy, then you can do with a simple It was lovely getting to know you!.

Things You Must Avoid

Here are some pointers that you should strictly stay away from so that you don't end up ruining a conversation with a guy you're interested in.

Killing the Mystery

Stay away from narrating your life history in one meeting. The key is to keep the mystery alive and let him discover you bit by bit. Also, while you are just a friend, do not involve him in your problems or sad stories, it will just make him uncomfortable.

Oversmart

While guys love a "beauty with brains" concept, they hate to be lectured or outwitted. Correcting him and forcefully bringing up heavy and intellectual topics will not help at all. It's not necessary to act dumb if you are smart and knowledgeable, but reduce the intensity of the conversation and make it light and friendly.

Finally, here are some lines that should never be used while talking to a guy you like:

"I am friends with all my ex-boyfriends": This will reflect that he is just a passing phase for you and you are setting the ground for a breakup already. It can also be misunderstood as a forceful attempt to make him jealous.

"I beat you again! Want to play another game?": In case you both are going out for games, play genuinely, but do not beat him every time, and insist that he plays again. This does not mean you should deliberately lose, but if he is really bad at the game, then it's better to leave from there or let him win. Guys don't like to be mocked at their weakness.

"I tell my best friend everything": Everyone knows you do, but there is no need to tell him that. This will make the guy nervous. He will think over every action and overanalyze each step. This will steal the spontaneity and ease from the conversation.

"Johnny Depp is the love of my life!": If a guy can't call Angelina Jolie "to die for", the girl can't also. Like I mentioned earlier, guys are more competitive than girls, and telling them that they are already fighting for the second place is not a good idea. The guy should feel he is all that you aspire, and let him bask in that glory.

To conclude, I'll consider bending my golden rule if only a little. If contrived scenarios and flirting lines just don't do it for you, just tell him that you like him; straight and simple. It takes courage, but remember, fortune favors the brave. What's the worst that could happen? In many cases, as in the case of the fabulous first days of attraction, the chase is more exhilarating than the win - what you say may make all the difference!

THE END

11431255R00058

Printed in Great Britain
by Amazon